HOME

ALEKSA AISHPUR • SACRED SEARCH FOR BELONGING

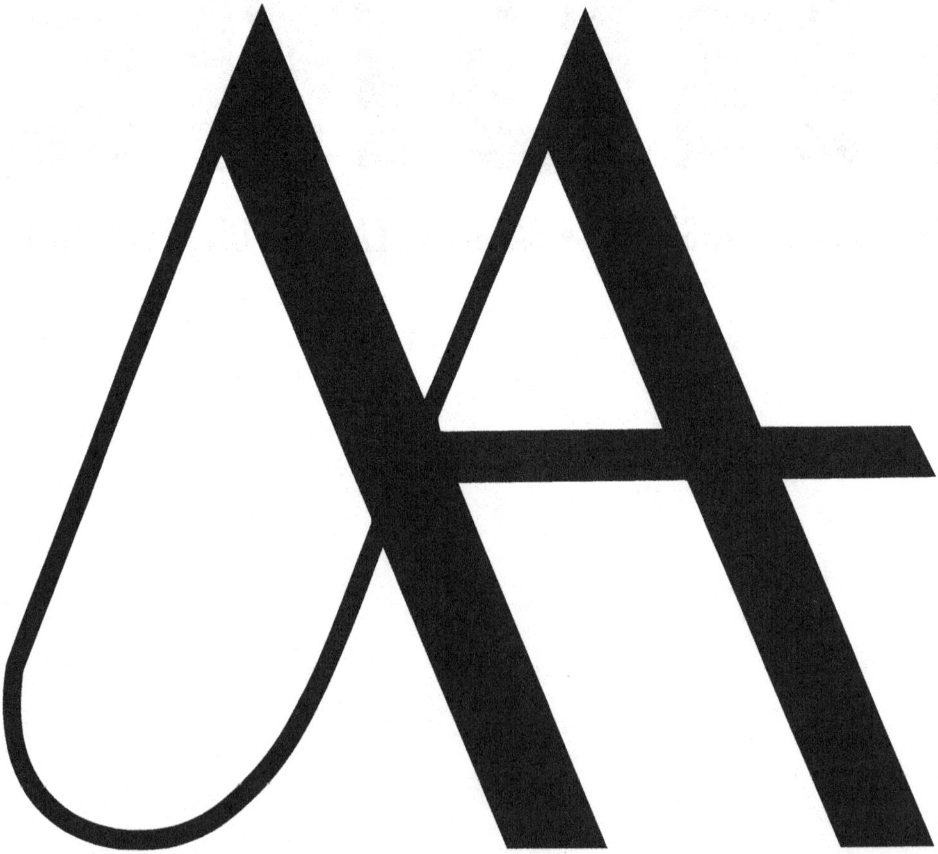

Home

Aleksa Aishpur

2023 © by Aleksa Aishpur

All rights reserved. Published 2023.

BIBLE SCRIPTURES

Printed in the United States of America

Spirit Media and our logos are trademarks of Spirit Media

🕊 SPIRIT MEDIA
www.spiritmedia.us
1249 Kildaire Farm Rd STE 112
Cary, NC 27511
1 (888) 800-3744

Books | Self- Help | Spiritual Self Help

Paperback (Colored) ISBN: 979-8-89307-008-8
Paperback (B&W) ISBN: 978-1-961614-92-5
Hardback ISBN (Colored): 978-1-961614-85-7
Hardback ISBN (B&W): 978-1-961614-91-8
Audiobook ISBN: 978-1-961614-86-4
eBook ISBN: 978-1-961614-83-3
Library of Congress Control Number: 2023919694

CONTENTS

INTRODUCTION

Hi, it's nice to meet you!

My name is Aleksa Aishpur. I have something that I want to share. It is a living book that has no ending. I authored it in this way so that those who read my book can create their own endings.

Each of us has different experiences and a different life that forms our present. My childhood was quite disturbing. My father died when I was a year old. My mother was left alone with my sister, who was eight years old at the time, and me. Those were the times of Perestroika. It was the dashing nineties when the government was changing. The Soviet Union was falling apart and there was complete lawlessness, gangs, and violence in the country. My mother was trying to survive the best way she could, while not losing hope and looking at life cheerfully. I am eternally grateful to her for this. Her inner strength taught me to love life no matter what!

Due to the complexity of the circumstances, I often lived with my grandmothers. They helped my mother on holidays, in winter, or when she was in trouble. As a result, I could move six times within one year. For a long time, I did not have a feeling of home. In fact, I would not know what it was like to call a place home until the age of thirty. I was looking for HOME. I would look into other people's windows, look at families, and get into unhealthy addictive relationships.

At one point, everything began to change. Thanks to the stories that I believe are from God, I began to understand that HOME is not a physical place and not people around me, but HOME is me, myself.

"He made known to us the mystery of his will according to his good pleasure, which he purposed in Christ, to be put into effect when the times reach their fulfillment—to bring unity to all things in heaven and on earth under Christ" (Ephesians 1:9-10, NIV).

I am a house for myself first of all, and for the loved ones to whom I open my house. It is my worldview, my philosophy of life, my foundation, and how I deal with everything that comes into my life. HOME is my inner balance, rest, peace, joy, and happiness. HOME is the place where I can be the real me, without masks, and without attempts to be like someone else or achieve something that is not me.

There is so much pain right now in my country, Ukraine. I am one of millions who have lost a physical home in 2022. I started to write this book and have visions from God in 2017, after the first war started in Eastern Ukraine in 2014. When I visited this place of pain and grief, I saw ruins of houses and lives. We gave bread to people in the gray zone near that place where there was active fighting. There were people fighting for bread. I had a million questions for God; it was hard to explain what I saw and the God that I knew at that time. I couldn't connect with it and I struggled with the fact that I couldn't help people. Month after month, I slowly started to have answers for my questions and for my misunderstanding of Jesus. During this period of war, many have lost family members, relatives, and friends. The number of deaths cannot be counted. And where is our home? Where is my house?

> "Consequently, you are no longer foreigners and strangers, but fellow citizens with God's people and also members of his household, built on the foundation of the apostles and prophets, with Christ Jesus himself as the chief cornerstone. In him the whole building is joined together and rises to become a holy temple in the Lord. And in him you too are being built together to become a dwelling in which God lives by his Spirit" (Ephesians 2:19-22, NIV).

How do I build it? Do I have to build it again if losing a home hurts so much? What if HOME is inside me, no matter where I am, whether there is a physically built house or a rented apartment or not, no matter who surrounds me? But what if HOME is not even people or loved ones, husbands, wives, or children? After all, these are the people who can die at any moment, and many in my country have lost their relatives.

But what if **HOME** is you and your spiritual life?

1

Ground Floor

GIFTS

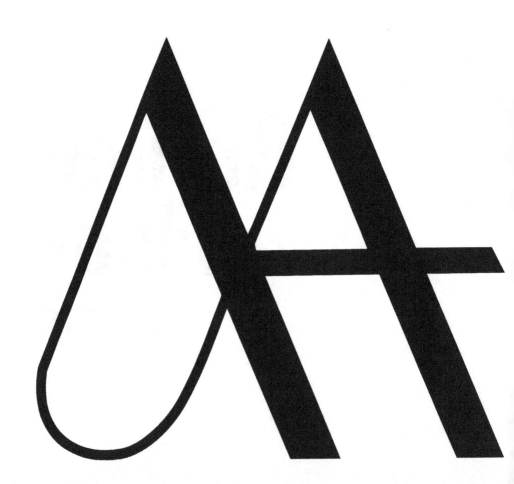

GIFTS

O nce, I stayed overnight at my friend, Vika's house. Her children had fallen asleep, and we talked for a long time. At the end of our evening, we decided to pray for each other, as we had both been through difficult times.

When she prayed, she had a vision, that I was soaring like an eagle, reaching the mountain tops. Then, I became human. I walked along the tops of those mountains and came to a castle. This was a heavenly palace around which God was taking me, showing me His home.

My friend said: "When I saw this vision I got goosebumps. I saw how God came down the stairs of His house to meet you. He was gently extending His hand inviting you to go higher and higher. Every movement was so easy. Every movement was filled with love. When you got to the top, you entered His house, where everything was one solid light. Everything was in white shades, and it felt as though the house was huge and boundless. His greatness was surely felt there. The Lord told you that you could look around His house. He said you could walk around and look at all the rooms. You entered one large room with a huge bed, and on the bed were enormous, fluffy white blankets. Like a small child, you began to somersault on those blankets. You were covered in them and being filled with His light! At the same time, there was an indescribable feeling of complete love, acceptance, care, and security!"

Hearing what she said, I went to bed feeling a little jealous that Vika was the one who saw this house, while I, the one that God brought into the house, didn't see it. I closed my eyes and said, "Lord, show me this house, the palace into which You led me. Show it to me, and tell me how I ended up inside."

First, I remembered what Vika said, and the vision began to fill with new details. It was simply breathtaking. The whole room was airy with high ceilings, huge windows, and transparent curtains. It had a white sofa, a fireplace, a white carpet, and a white chest with drawers. It was very spacious, but cozy at the same time. It felt fresh in the room, and the light curtains were blowing in the breeze. In the vases were snow-white flowers—all kinds that I had seen in my life, but at the same time, were unknown to me. This tangible breeze was so gentle that I enjoyed it with my eyes closed. Then, it was as if I had passed through this room when God led me to a beautiful staircase, lining the entire window. We began to climb it, and the picture ended.

It was the room of acceptance where I feel like myself—like a real me without borders or other people's patterns, absolutely loved by God. No pressure to be good or bad, obedient or not.

Freedom. No anxious thoughts.

I accept myself and feel comfortable with myself. It looks like the hands of a person that you love and who loves you is hugging you (mom, child, father, partner, friend, or husband). It looks like you have wings and are ready to fly and nobody can stop you! It is very important to have inner lightness, simplicity, and lightheartedness. Acceptance is what gives us a fresh look at life's circumstances and the inspiration to move on.

I encourage you to take a break to answer these questions:

QUESTIONS

01

02

03

04

05

Do you have a friend or a partner, someone with whom you can pray together, share your thoughts, and support each other?

_____

_____

_____

_____

What are some things in your life that you need to accept?

_____

_____

_____

_____

What makes you feel light-hearted?

_____

_____

_____

_____

What do you need to change about your mindset to make your life simpler and more happy?

_____

_____

_____

_____

Do you use your imagination to see something helpful from God?

_____

_____

_____

_____

2

Second Floor

FOUNDATION

FOUNDATION

Closing my eyes again, I found myself on the second floor of a house with a corridor leading into rooms in all different directions. It was a bit like a hotel, yet this floor had coziness and beauty, which created the feeling of home. The hall was completely covered in red stones. There was a red carpet on the floor, and it stretched all the way down the hall. The lobby, which led into the hall, had a pinkish-red carpet, red sofas, and places on which there were raw red crystals. The carpet was round and large, and the furniture was dark and wooden. Everything was amazingly laid out in such a beautiful way.

The ceilings were high and reached up to about three meters (about ten feet). The windows were bright with wide curtains, transparent in white and red. There were chandeliers and lamps all covered in red stones. Even though I didn't know the names of all the different stones, I was amazed by their beauty. The floor and the hall were completely made of stone. It felt like walking on solid red stones. Some places were like a mosaic, and other places were simply huge pieces of transparent red stone. I wanted to enjoy the atmosphere so much that I lay down on the sofa. It was a retro style sofa with red velvet upholstery. The color was so brilliant that I could not take my eyes off of it. Since the room was flooded with light, the precious stones shimmered with incredibly bright and beautiful hues. It seems to me that I fell asleep for a while from an overabundance of emotions. It was like swimming in a pool. Fatigue left my body, and I was filled with complete satisfaction.

When I came to my senses, I noticed that colors shimmered outside the windows as if something was being reflected. I jumped off the couch and ran to the window. I closed my eyes because it was so bright, and then I gradually opened them, squinting as I got used to the light. From my new vantage point, I now recognized this home I had been in was a castle, completely covered in precious stones.

It was so huge and so bright from the reflection of the sun, that my eyes had to adjust to the light before I could truly see this beautiful castle in its entirety.

Overall, the castle was huge, with six or more floors and high towers. I recognized the two bottom floors where I had been, and I longed to explore the other floors. It looked like it was made of glass. But it was stone reflecting the sun, creating an illusion of glass while hiding the rooms inside like a secret. All kinds of other precious stones and pearls were embedded in this transparent stone so beautifully that I wouldn't be able to draw or capture it in any way. I looked up and saw beautiful high towers.

When my eyes looked down, I suddenly realized that I was very, very high! This castle was on top of a mountain so high, I could see clouds below my feet. The clouds cleared, and I saw the beauty of the Earth and its nature down below. The green fields, rivers, mountains, sky, and clouds looked incredibly beautiful at that height. I was overcome by emotions of boundless delight. Everything delighted me. I turned around and looked back into the red room. It was beautiful—all scarlet. To me, it looked like the power of atonement for the sins of man—the power of the shed blood of Jesus Christ. It was then I realized, this floor with the red hall was only the starting point for the journey to other rooms—the depths of revelation.

Red stones are rubies. I started looking in the Bible to see if I could find rubies described somewhere, and I found them in Isaiah 54:

"'Though the mountains be shaken and the hills be removed, yet my unfailing love for you will not be shaken nor my covenant of peace be removed,' says the Lord, who has compassion on you. 'Afflicted city, lashed by storms and not comforted, **I will rebuild you with stones of turquoise, your foundations with lapis lazuli. I will make your battlements of rubies, your gates of sparkling jewels, and all your walls of precious stones.** All your children will be taught by the Lord, and great will be their peace. In righteousness you will be established: Tyranny will be far from you; you will have nothing to fear. Terror will be far removed; it will not come near you. If anyone does attack you, it will not be my doing; whoever attacks you will surrender to you.'"

"'No weapon forged against you will prevail, and you will refute every tongue that accuses you. This is the heritage of the servants of the Lord, and this is their vindication from me,' declares the Lord.'" (Isaiah 54:10-15, 17, NIV)

Then, I found rubies again in the book of Revelation:

"I saw the Holy City, the new Jerusalem, coming down out of heaven from God, prepared as a bride beautifully dressed for her husband. And I heard a loud voice from the throne saying, 'Look! God's dwelling place is now among the people, and he will dwell with them. They will be his people, and God himself will be with them and be their God. 'He will wipe every tear from their eyes. There will be no more death' or mourning or crying or pain, for the old order of things has passed away."

He who was seated on the throne said, "I am making everything new!" Then he said, "Write this down, for these words are trustworthy and true."

'He said to me: "It is done. I am the Alpha and the Omega, the Beginning and the End. To the thirsty I will give water without cost from the spring of the water of life. Those who are victorious will inherit all this, and I will be their God and they will be my children.'"

"And he carried me away in the Spirit to a mountain great and high, and showed me the Holy City, Jerusalem, coming down out of heaven from God. It shone with the glory of God, and its brilliance was like that of a very precious jewel, like a jasper, clear as crystal."

"The wall was made of jasper, and the city of pure gold, as pure as glass. The foundations of the city walls were decorated with every kind of precious stone. The first foundation was jasper, the second sapphire, the third agate, the fourth emerald, the fifth onyx, the sixth ruby, the seventh chrysolite, the eighth beryl, the ninth topaz, the tenth turquoise, the eleventh jacinth, and the twelfth amethyst. The twelve gates were twelve pearls, each gate made of a single pearl. The great street of the city was of gold, as pure as transparent glass.

I did not see a temple in the city, because the Lord God Almighty and the Lamb are its temple. **The city does not need the sun or the moon to shine on it, for the glory of God gives it light, and the Lamb is its lamp."** (Revelation 21:2-7; 10-11; 18-23, NIV).

I believe that these passages hold promises in the life of every person. And I believe that we can live on Earth as in heaven by finding the heavenly home within us and holding on to the promises of God, as we see the reality of His promises at work in our lives.

Establish a peaceful atmosphere, and set aside some time to respond to these questions:

QUESTIONS

01

02

03

04

05

What promises has God given you?

_____
_____
_____
_____

Do you value God's Word and His promises as if they were rubies?

_____
_____
_____
_____

How did the experience in the red room and the view outside affect you?

_____
_____
_____
_____

Can you draw personal connections from this description and the biblical passages?

_____
_____
_____
_____

What is treasure for you?

_____
_____
_____
_____

3

First
Room
LIVE SOUND

LIVE SOUND

When I opened the door, a huge green meadow opened up in front of me. On it grew tall, soft grass and tall, leafy trees. They were similar to each other in height, resembling poplars in shape. The glade was flooded with light, and the sky was soft blue with small, white clouds. I wanted to lie down on the grass. Once I lay down, I began to hear a sound. It was so unusual! At that moment, I realized that the air was thick. I also realized I was not breathing in just the air, but something was filling me. The noise of leaves, grass, birds, insects, my heartbeat, and my breathing—all of it merged. It felt like the sound was alive.

Turning my head, I saw a crystal. It was the size of a coffee table. This crystal was transparent blue like a diamond, and it was shining. At some point, it rose into the air and crumbled into many crystals the size of my palm, hovering in the air. Then, each of them at one moment crumbled into even smaller crystals—the size of a baby's palm. And then into smaller and smaller ones. Each time the crystals became smaller and smaller and smaller until I stopped seeing them and they became air—part of the sound, the melody, part of what I breathed, part of what filled me, part of who I am. I began to understand that the sound and the visible realm are one. The senses carry the same message. I am filled with it. I do not need to look for it. It is inside me!

Bible Scriptures:

"In the beginning was the Word, and the Word was with God, **and the Word was God**" (John 1:1, NIV).

"Day after day they pour forth speech; night after night they reveal knowledge. They have no speech, they use no words; no sound is heard from them. Yet their voice goes out into all the earth, their words to the ends of the world" (Psalms 19:2-5, NIV).

Give yourself a brief break and then answer these questions:

QUESTIONS

01

02

03

04

05

How does the transformation of the crystal into smaller pieces resonate with you? What do you think it symbolizes?

_____

_____

_____

_____

Have you ever thought that every moment of your life, you are breathing and filled with God?

_____

_____

_____

_____

When have you felt God's Word near to you and deep in your heart?

_____

_____

_____

_____

Do you believe God's Word is powerful and alive?

_____

_____

_____

_____

How can you cultivate a deeper awareness of the connection between sound, sight, and your own inner being in your daily life?

_____

_____

_____

_____

4

Second Room

WAR

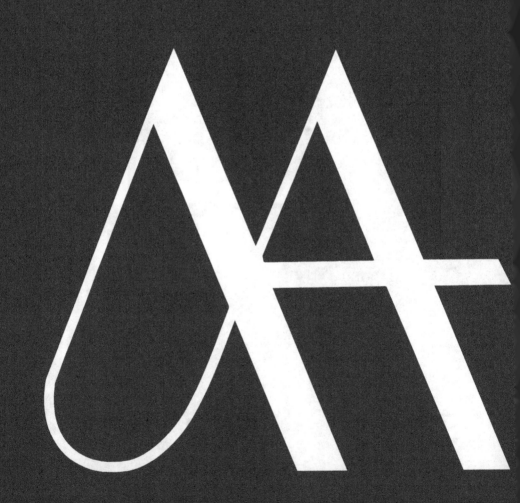

WAR

I t was my usual day. When I got home, I wanted to go and pray. I just closed my eyes and found myself in front of another door. The thrill of anticipation filled me, so I opened the door. I was a little upset. I expected to see nature, something pleasant. In general, after seeing a huge space outside the door, I thought I would see something like that again. But I saw a small room of fifteen square meters. Everything was black and white, clear, and angular. There was an oblique window in the middle of the wall and two corners: the right one at the top and the left one at the bottom were sixty degrees, and the other two were ninety degrees.

The walls were painted in black and white triangles. Near the window stood a very small, round, and modern black table. On it lay a huge, thick book with a black cover, white pages, and black text, with black and white photographs. I was very attracted to the book, so I went to it. My surprise was simply overwhelming. It was the book of wars throughout the history of mankind from very ancient to modern. I started flipping through it, and a great sadness began to fill my heart.

I hate war. In 2014, when hostilities began in Ukraine for the first time in the Donbas Region, I went there with a small team to deliver bread to people near the gray zone. This zone was a few hours from the city of Slovyansk, the city where the worst battles were, and the part that got shelled from time to time. Shops and banks did not work there. Entire infrastructures were destroyed. The villages on the way to our destination were completely destroyed. We saw houses without roofs or walls and fences with bullet holes.

They told stories about these houses where people died, and they described the type of shelling that was used. They shared about how children saw their dying parents (or vice versa) and how sometimes entire families died. But what shocked me the most was still ahead. We brought bread in a minibus and filled the whole car with bread—

no bags, just a bunch of loaves of bread. We were handing out bread to people—we didn't wash our hands, we just gave it as it was, and two men started fighting for a loaf of bread. I looked on in horror, as I saw people become like animals. Others were swearing because someone got two loaves, and someone got only one.

This was forever imprinted in my memory. It was scary, not only because of death and devastation, but also because those who survived turned wild and became like animals trying to meet their very basic needs, like food. Therefore, when a full-scale war began in Ukraine in 2022, I fled on the first day the war started. I had already seen what would happen, and I understood that it would last far longer than just one month.

In this room, hatred rose in my heart. It began to cloud my heart and mind, like the darkness that covered me. And then I felt that God was with me. He fully understood me and all my feelings. He does not plan wars, but the human heart plans wars. Man goes against man, like the first people on Earth: Cain against Abel. They killed each other out of envy, desire for power, and greed. God does not go against the will of man; He created us to have freedom to choose. Choose life or death, good or evil.

What impressed me in this room was that God said that He turns all this suffering into good. He makes progress out of devastation, happiness out of grief, and laughter out of tears. All wars, for example, the First and Second World Wars, lead to progress: strong leaps in science, medicine, etc. Why? Because God puts in our hearts the desire for life, growth, happiness, and deep values. Life is not just life on Earth. It is not just living our daily human life, but it is something more sublime and infinite than a person thinks or sees. This is what a person in crisis feels like. War is a crisis that, thanks to God, becomes a new stage or springboard for development.

In this room, the understanding came that death is not the end for the individual. It is the end for the body and flesh but not for the soul and spirit: the mind, intellect, emotions, and the ability to communicate with God. Awareness of this does not limit us to only focusing on injustice but opens up opportunities to think big. To look into the depths of the meaning of life and not to waste time here on Earth, but to seek God—His voice, His revelations, and His will—and to follow Him, as He was, is, and is coming. In heaven, the war for our souls has been going on for millennia without end. And every time God wins. This is how we overcome and win in our personal lives.

Bible Scriptures:

" . . . I have set before you life and death, blessings and curses. Now choose life, so that you and your children may live and that you may love the Lord your God, listen to his voice, and hold fast to him. For the Lord is your life, and he will give you many years . . . " (Deuteronomy 30:19-20, NIV).

"Abel kept flocks, and Cain worked the soil. In the course of time Cain brought some of the fruits of the soil as an offering to the Lord. And Abel also brought an offering—fat portions from some of the firstborn of his flock. The Lord looked with favor on Abel and his offering, but on Cain and his offering he did not look with favor. So Cain was very angry, and his face was downcast. Then the Lord said to Cain, 'Why are you angry? Why is your face downcast? If you do what is right, will you not be accepted? **But if you do not do what is right, sin is crouching at your door; it desires to have you, but you must rule over it.'** Now Cain said to his brother Abel, 'Let's go out to the field.' While they were in the field, Cain attacked his brother Abel and killed him" (Genesis 4:2-8, NIV).

"The Spirit of the Sovereign Lord is on me, because the Lord has anointed me to proclaim good news to the poor. He has sent me to bind up the brokenhearted, to proclaim freedom for the captives and release from darkness for the prisoners, to proclaim the year of the Lord's favor and the day of vengeance of our God, to comfort all who mourn, and provide for those who grieve in Zion—to bestow on them a crown of beauty instead of ashes, the oil of joy instead of mourning, and a garment of praise instead of a spirit of despair. They will be called oaks of righteousness, a planting of the Lord for the display of his splendor. **They will rebuild the ancient ruins and restore the places long devastated; they will renew the ruined cities that have been devastated for generations.** Strangers will shepherd your flocks; foreigners will work your fields and vineyards. And you will be called priests of the Lord, you will be named ministers of our God. You will feed on the wealth of nations, and in their riches you will boast. Instead of your shame you will receive a double portion, and instead of disgrace you will rejoice in your inheritance. And so you will inherit a double portion in your land, and everlasting joy will be yours. "For I, the Lord, love justice; I hate robbery and wrongdoing. In my faithfulness I will reward my people and make an everlasting covenant with them. **Their descendants will be known among the nations and their offspring among the peoples. All who see them will acknowledge that they are a people the Lord has blessed"** (Isaiah 61:1-9, NIV).

"Then war broke out in heaven. Michael and his angels fought against the dragon, and the dragon and his angels fought back. But he was not strong enough, and they lost their place in heaven. The great dragon was hurled down—that ancient serpent called the devil, or Satan, who leads the whole world astray. He was hurled to the earth, and his angels with him. Then I heard a loud voice in heaven say: '**Now have come the salvation and the power and the kingdom of our God,** and the authority of his Messiah. For the accuser of our brothers and sisters, who accuses them before our God day and night, has been hurled down. They triumphed over him by the blood of the Lamb and by the word of their testimony; they did not love their lives so much as to shrink from death. Therefore rejoice, you heavens and you who dwell in them! But woe to the earth and the sea, because the devil has gone down to you! **He is filled with fury, because he knows that his time is short**'" (Revelation 12:7-12, NIV).

"Be alert and of sober mind. Your enemy the devil prowls around like a roaring lion looking for someone to devour. **Resist him, standing firm in the faith**, because you know that the family of believers throughout the world is undergoing the same kind of sufferings. And the God of all grace, who called you to his eternal glory in Christ, after you have suffered a little while, will himself **restore you and make you strong, firm and steadfast"** (1 Peter 5:8-10, NIV).

Find some place to reflect and respond to these questions at your own pace:

QUESTIONS

01

02

03

04

05

When you think about your own personal suffering in life, what comes to mind? How does it make you feel?

_____

_____

_____

_____

Do you believe God can use suffering to bring about good?

_____

_____

_____

_____

Do you believe that God plans wars?

_____

_____

_____

_____

Do you believe that God prepares bad times for us to teach us?

_____

_____

_____

_____

If He is not preparing bad times for you, can you imagine now how He sympathizes with you and how He goes with you through all your difficulties? What does it look like?

_____

_____

_____

_____

5

Third Room
PAST

PAST

Once, my heart was sad. I began to pray, closed my eyes, and found myself in front of another door. When I opened it, I was surprised. I got into a small retro room. The wallpaper was beige, in a small peach-colored pattern. It had an old window with a wooden window frame, a wooden window sill, and a curtain made of thin, beige, crocheted fabric. A small antique mirror hung on one wall, and opposite it stood a small wrought-iron round table and a chair. I wanted to sit on that chair. On the table was a crocheted napkin and a vase with a narrow neck. There was one flower in the vase, tilted slightly to the side.

As soon as I started walking to the chair, I realized that I was also dressed in retro-style clothes from the thirties or forties: a long dress, high-waisted, with a thin belt at the waist, a smooth shirt with a collar, and a brooch. My hair was pulled in a bun. When I was sitting on the chair, my face was right in front of the mirror, and I saw my reflection. At that moment, I realized that the past is neither good nor bad. It has shaped our thinking and our view of many things. It can affect our lives emotionally today. The past is what was and will never be again. It cannot be repeated. And it affects exactly as much of our present-day lives as we allow it to. Often, we are not fully aware of the influence of the past on our lives.

Patterns of behavior, repetitive events, or unsuccessful relationships are what we unconsciously reproduce. This is because in childhood, we learned that such events are love. For example, a girl who was beaten by her father will choose a man who beats her. Why? Because probably for her, it is love. Or if you lived in a family where one of the parents was addicted to alcohol (or had some kind of addiction), then you will probably choose the same relationship in adulthood because, if there is an addicted person nearby, it will feel like love to you. Specialists help us get out of such cycles or models—people like counselors, psychologists, coaches, and mentors. It is sometimes difficult to find such models on your own. The most important thing is this: Don't be afraid to look into the past, even for traumatic events. Things like unforgiveness, envy, anger, and wrong expectations spoil our present. If you don't understand why you have a similar response year after year, you must deal with the past. It is the past that brings us either freedom or slavery!

I once heard that the human heart is divided into four parts. The first one is what I know about myself and what others know. The second is what I know about myself and others do not know. The third is what I do not know but others know, because they see me from the side. The fourth is a part that neither I know nor other people know, but God knows. Therefore, it is important to let the right people into your life, and let God into your life in order to acquire freedom. Recognize yourself and become whole—moving in your destiny, having peace in your heart, and living a happy life.

Bible Scriptures:

"Now the Lord is the Spirit, and **where the Spirit of the Lord is, there is freedom**" (2 Corinthians 3:17, NIV).

Do not be afraid to look into the past; it's like looking into a mirror and seeing a reflection, but in order to understand that the mirror is the past, not the present, go through the pain to victory. The difficult things we have experienced in the past prepare us for the future. The past should not be forgotten, it should be made an incentive for change—a quality foundation. You form the present, creating it with God's help and His promptings in the form of "open doors," new opportunities and people who help you.

"For **I know the plans I have for you,'** declares the Lord, **'plans to prosper you** and not to harm you, plans to give you hope and a future. Then you will call on me and come and pray to me, and I will listen to you. You will seek me and find me when you seek me with all your heart.'" (Jeremiah 29:11-13, NIV)

Relax and take a short break, then answer these questions:

QUESTIONS

01

02

03

04

44

How are you letting the past change you?

_____
_____
_____
_____
_____
_____

Is the past powerful for you today?

_____
_____
_____
_____
_____
_____

Are you falling into slavery to the past or are you moving forward in freedom?

_____
_____
_____
_____
_____
_____

Do you believe that God has plans to prosper you?

_____
_____
_____
_____
_____
_____

6

Fourth Room

STORM

STORM

Opening the door, I found myself on the beach and going to the water where I saw Jesus. He held out His hand to me and we walked on the water. We went deep, but did not dive. The water was ankle-deep, but due to the fact that the clouds were dragging on, the waves began to rise and reached my knees and waist. Although a storm was approaching and the sea was getting very rough, it was not scary at all. It felt like I was walking on glass and could not drown. We had already moved far from the coastline, and there was a great depth. Somewhere at a distance from me, there was a wrecked ship. It sat on a small, rocky stone.

When I was standing far from shore, Jesus disappeared somewhere, and I felt that I needed to lie on the water. It was strange because there was already an incredible storm around, and the waves became huge above me. From time to time, the water hit my face unpleasantly. But I felt such confidence and peace that I just took it and lay down on the water, spreading my arms to the sides like a starfish. I was lying as if on glass. It was cool, but not icy, and I did not feel cold.

The waves periodically covered me.

Drops fell from the sky and the wind blew, but I experienced incredible peace. I knew Jesus brought me here and nothing terrible could happen. Besides, this storm would pass, and the fact of my experience would not change anything. If I tried to swim against the current, I could die because the sea was raging.

I heard the voice of God inside me saying, "calm."

If everything around is stormy—so much so that panic sets in—you need to enter the "internal calm." Calm down, wait for the storm to end, and then make a decision. If we don't make peace with a past decision we've made, we can greatly harm ourselves and crash like a ship on a rock. But by calming down and listening to our inner voice, we can find a way out. On the contrary, if we panic during storms, we can drown. Hasty decisions based on fear and panic can ruin our lives. If we have no strength (or when we fear, panic or doubt), we need to admit it, wait a bit until the storm subsides, and then move on in peace.

Bible Scripture:

"Do you not know? Have you not heard? The Lord is the everlasting God, the Creator of the ends of the earth. He will not grow tired or weary, and his understanding no one can fathom. **He gives strength to the weary and increases the power of the weak. Even youths grow tired and weary, and young men stumble and fall; but those who hope in the Lord will renew their strength.** They will soar on wings like eagles; they will run and not grow weary, they will walk and not faint" (Isaiah 40:28-31, NIV).

Relax and share your thoughts on these questions:

QUESTIONS

01

02

03

04

What do you turn to in times of trouble?

_____

_____

_____

_____

_____

_____

Where do you find peace?

_____

_____

_____

_____

_____

_____

How do you find strength and renewal in the Lord during wearisome times?

_____

_____

_____

_____

_____

_____

What are some ways you can find God's presence in a storm?

_____

_____

_____

_____

_____

_____

7

Fifth
Room
SEASONS

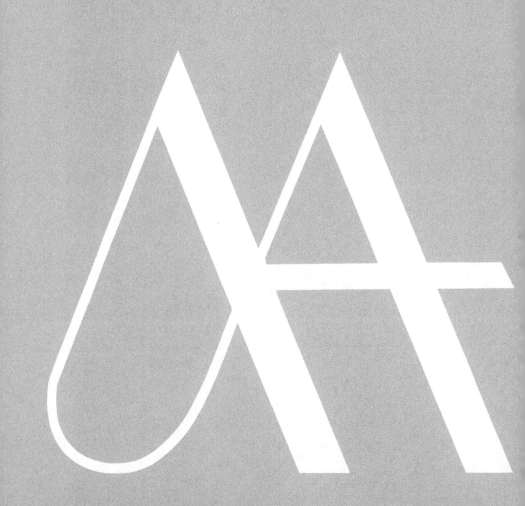

SEASONS

I closed my eyes, began to pray, and ended up in front of another door. Opening it, I saw a huge garden in which there were many fruits. Many people were working in the garden. Some picked fruit, others carried them, others made juice from them, some made jam, and there were a couple that dried them. Children ran around in herds, eating all the goodies from the trees. I heard the sound of loud laughter, dialogue, and voices of men, women, and children.

I understood that this was my garden. Someone was constantly coming up to me, asking for advice on how and what to do, what I thought would be right, where to use what, and how to distribute the fruit collected from the trees. "Make juice out of these . . . give these to the orphanage . . . these go to the store . . . make jam from these . . . " So, day after day passed in this way. Finally, the moment came when the fruits were almost harvested and there were fewer and fewer people.

I was left alone.

I sat on a stool and watched the leaves fall.

Yellow leaves were falling.

Empty.

The hardest part after a harvest is waiting for the next harvest, since there is only a single field—your life. After the harvest comes the joy of the harvest, but after a while, it becomes different. You have to wait for the next one. The harvest comes at its own time, and the moments of waiting are painful. This is also because when the harvest is in progress (besides the satisfaction of reaping fruit), a lot of people surround you, they work with you, do something, and spend time with you.

Then everyone disperses, and you experience loneliness because you do not understand why people have disappeared or where they have gone. And if you do not understand this, then you can fall into depression or a state of loneliness: melancholy and unsatisfied. Or this time can provide rest for a person—an opportunity to gain strength before new work and before the arrival of the new harvest. Nothing is lost. At this very moment, the Earth is gaining strength to bring even more fruit, and so are we.

Allow yourself to wait and yearn, to be sad and bored, because this time will give you an incentive for greater growth.

Bible Scripture:

"'For everything there is a season, and **a time for every matter under heaven:** A time to be born, and a time to die; a time to plant, and a time to pluck up what is planted; a time to kill, and a time to heal; a time to break down, and a time to build up; a time to weep, and a time to laugh; a time to mourn, and a time to dance; a time to cast away stones, and a time to gather stones together; a time to embrace, and a time to refrain from embracing; a time to seek, and a time to lose; a time to keep, and a time to cast away; a time to tear, and a time to sew; a time to keep silence, and a time to speak; a time to love, and a time to hate; a time for war, and a time for peace.

What gain has the worker from his toil? I have seen the business that God has given to the children of man to be busy with. He has made everything beautiful in its time. Also, he has put eternity into man's heart, yet so that he cannot find out what God has done from the beginning to the end. I perceived that there is nothing better for them than to be joyful and to do good as long as they live; also that everyone should eat and drink and take pleasure in all his toil—this is the gift of God'" (Ecclesiastes 3:1-13, ESV).

Allow yourself a short break to relax and reflect, then tackle these questions with renewed focus:

QUESTIONS

01

02

03

04

What kind of season are you in right now?

_____

_____

_____

_____

_____

Are you waiting for something?

_____

_____

_____

_____

_____

How do you find satisfaction and joy in your work and daily life, even during periods of waiting?

_____

_____

_____

_____

_____

How do you see God using this time of waiting to grow your faith and give you strength?

_____

_____

_____

_____

_____

8

Sixth Room

YOURS

YOURS

It was the work Jesus was doing on the cross. He calls us to be where He is. He calls us to the rooms prepared for each of us. Ask Him where He is now, what room you are in, and at what point in time.

I suggest you go to your room now. Close your eyes for a few minutes, and think about what room you are entering. Turn on your imagination. Ask God to help you see. Write or draw on a piece of paper, in a gadget, or here. It can be just a thought, a picture, or a plot.

Bible Scripture:

"My Father's house has many rooms. If it were not so, would I have told you that I go to prepare a place for you? And if I go and prepare a place for you, I will come again and will take you to myself, that where I am, you may be also" (John 14:2-3, ESV).

Take a moment to reflect and respond to these questions:

QUESTIONS

01

02

03

04

05

Is what you saw similar to your time now?

_____

_____

_____

_____

_____

What season is your life in right now?

_____

_____

_____

_____

_____

What do you feel in this room?

_____

_____

_____

_____

_____

Do you need to act now or wait?

_____

_____

_____

_____

_____

What did you think about what you saw, understood, or realized?

_____

_____

_____

_____

_____

Let's encourage others to get closer to God together and see their own HOME inside!

I ask you to send me your story. Share your story with me, and I'll feature it on our website and social media platforms. You'll have the option to be tagged on social media or remain anonymous.

Simply follow this link at **aishpur.com** or **scan the QR code** to submit your story.

9

Seventh Room

MIRROR

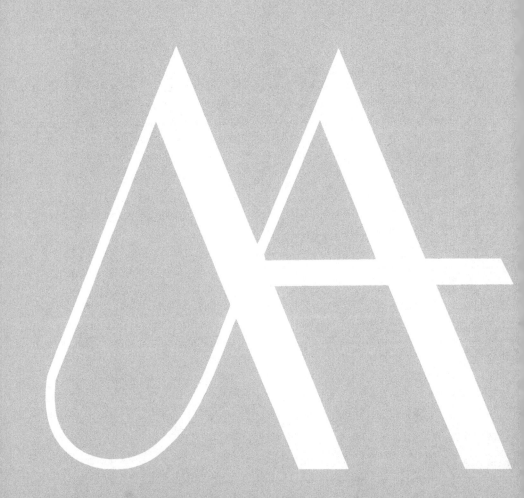

MIRROR

It was a bedtime prayer.

I saw myself already pushing the doorknob and entering a room where there were a lot of people in a small amount of space. Everyone was holding a mirror in front of them, and each mirror was distorted or dirty in different ways. Three or four people came up to the window and directed the mirrors at the sun. They were reflecting the sunlight, but with their backs on other people. It was as if they saw nothing but the sun.

I was embarrassed as I saw myself in different mirrors.

I looked different.

I understood the way people see me, and what they see. They see through the prism of their vision of the world, like a projection. We see ourselves in other people. In addition, my mirror also turned out to be dim. This means, when people look at me, they see through my dim mirror, and their vision is also superimposed on mine. I hope I didn't confuse you, but this is a distorted reality of what we are and what kind of people we are.

I was wondering who these people were near the window and why they were pointing their mirrors at the sun. Then, I remembered this verse from the Bible, in 2 Corinthians 3:18. "And we all, who with unveiled faces contemplate the Lord's glory, **are being transformed into his image with ever-increasing glory,** which comes from the Lord, who is the Spirit."

So they cleaned their mirrors, directing them towards the light—the sun.

Bible Scriptures:

"Do not conform to the pattern of this world, but be transformed by the renewing of your mind. Then you will be able to test and approve what God's will is—his good, pleasing and perfect will" (Romans 12:2, NIV).

"Why do you look at the speck of sawdust in your brother's eye and pay no attention to the plank in your own eye? How can you say to your brother, 'Brother, let me take the speck out of your eye,' when you yourself fail to see the plank in your own eye? You hypocrite, first take the plank out of your eye, and then you will see clearly to remove the speck from your brother's eye" (Matthew 7:3-5, NIV).

"No good tree bears bad fruit, nor does a bad tree bear good fruit. Each tree is recognized by its own fruit. People do not pick figs from thorn bushes, or grapes from briers. A good man brings good things out of the good stored up in his heart, and an evil man brings evil things out of the evil stored up in his heart. For the mouth speaks what the heart is full of" (Luke 6:41-45, NIV).

Take the opportunity to reflect before answering these questions:

QUESTIONS

01

02

03

04

How do you see the people around you? Are they good or are they always bad? Do you criticize others?

_____

_____

_____

_____

_____

How do you see yourself? Do you enjoy yourself? Do you enjoy your life?

_____

_____

_____

_____

_____

If you do not enjoy your life, do you know of any people who can help you? Ask God to show you or remind someone.

_____

_____

_____

_____

_____

How does the condition of our hearts and minds affect the way we perceive ourselves and others?

_____

_____

_____

_____

_____

10

Eighth
Room
INHERITANCE

INHERITANCE

When I entered the room, I saw a crystal in the middle of the room. This stone was exactly like a diamond. It shimmered from the light coming from the ceiling above it. The whole room was filled with bright reflections of the shimmering colors. At one point, I became this crystal. I saw how pure I was and how beautifully I shone in different directions, reflecting the light. But suddenly, I felt uncomfortable. I felt that I was not so pure, and I felt ashamed that I glowed so beautifully, while there was still sin and dirt inside. I felt that I was unworthy of either being a crystal or having it.

I, again, looked from the side, and saw that the crystal was standing on the cross, at the top of the cross.

I immediately remembered the verse, John 13:10 (NIV)—**"Those who have had a bath need only to wash their feet; their whole body is clean.** And you are clean, though not every one of you."

The cross and the remembrance of the cross is the washing of our dirty feet. After all, no one who loves God sins on purpose or for evil, but everyone does get dirty sometimes. Our repentance cleanses us so that we reflect the true and pure light, giving us dignity and confidence.

Each of us is a child of God—the Creator of everything and everyone.

After that, I again found myself in the place of the crystal, and I saw myself standing with my feet on the horizontal beam of the cross. God said that even if you had no doctrine, no inheritance like the Jews, or could not build on true principles, you have an inheritance through the Holy Spirit! God has everything for you!

You stand strong.

Then the vision ended.

Bible Scriptures:

"Therefore, **there is now no condemnation for those who are in Christ Jesus,** because through Christ Jesus the law of the Spirit who gives life has set you free from the law of sin and death. For what the law was powerless to do because it was weakened by the flesh, God did by sending his own Son in the likeness of sinful flesh to be a sin offering" (Romans 8:1-3, NIV).

"Therefore, since we have a great high priest who has ascended into heaven, Jesus the Son of God, let us hold firmly to the faith we profess. For we do not have a high priest who is unable to empathize with our weaknesses, but we have one who has been tempted in every way, just as we are—yet he did not sin. Let us then approach God's throne of grace with confidence, so that we may receive mercy and find grace to help us in our time of need" (Hebrews 4:14-16, NIV).

Pause briefly, relax your mind, and respond to these questions:

QUESTIONS

01

02

03

04

If you know you have an inheritance from God, how does that change your life?

_____

_____

_____

_____

_____

What do you do when you sin?

_____

_____

_____

_____

_____

How does repentance cleanse us and allow us to reflect true and pure light?

_____

_____

_____

_____

_____

How does reflecting on these verses and the experience in the eighth room impact your understanding of God's forgiveness and love?

_____

_____

_____

_____

_____

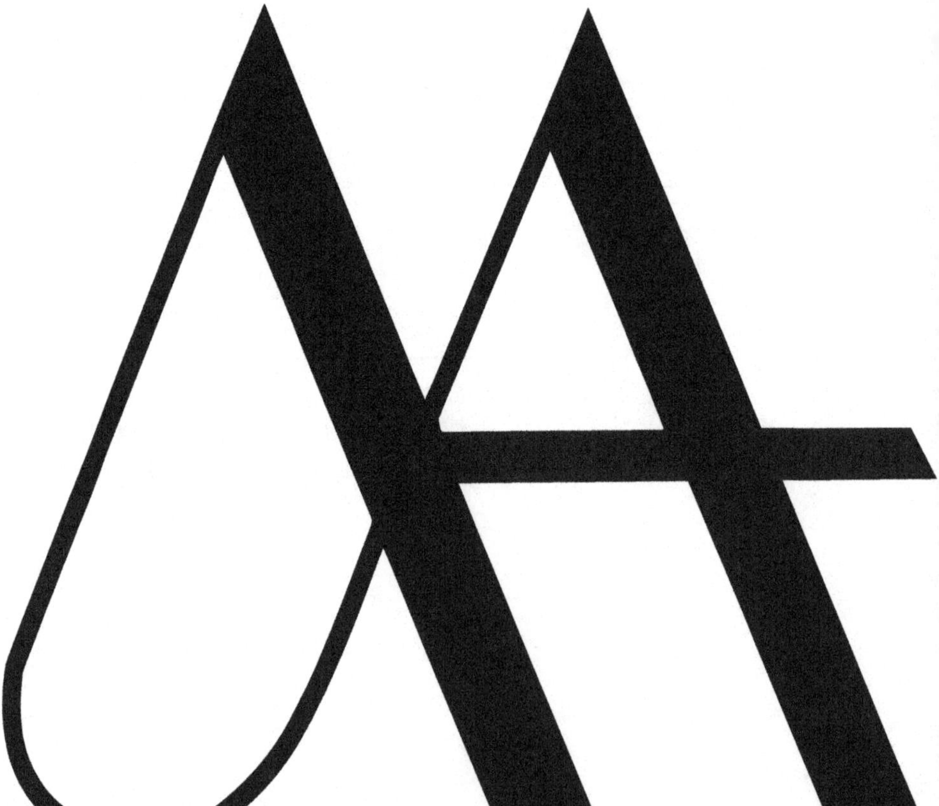

11

Ninth Room
CHANGES

CHANGES

One of the meanings of black is change. It's when something ends, and something else begins. This is the last room in this book, and this is the room I have been in for the past few years. But, this is not the last room for me or for every reader of this book. We open rooms one after another throughout our lives, getting to know ourselves, God, and the spiritual world better and better.

I opened the door, and found myself in absolute darkness. It was so dark that out of fear, I began to think of everything. I was so overcome with fears that I felt that I would break (since in the dream I was a crystal). I suddenly imagined I was falling off a cliff, and there was an endless abyss below. Then, I thought that some animals would eat me there, or people would mock me as if I was waiting for an attack. As a result, the idea came to me to shout loudly into the darkness in order to measure the space. I screamed loudly and realized that I was in a small room with a floor, walls, and a ceiling. This was something understandable, I just didn't see it. What I don't see doesn't mean danger.

For several years, I could not interpret this room. I even considered not including it in this book. It was only after a while that it made sense to me. If you abruptly enter a very brightly lit room, then for a while you seem to go blind. The room is so bright that you can't see anything, and there is darkness in your eyes. Then gradually, after a long while, light appears.

When we are close to God, we may think that He is not there or that He is far away, since in His light we can be blinded and not see anything for a while. And, only after a while do we understand how close He was to us throughout this period.

Bible Scriptures:

This is the message we have heard from him and declare to you:

"God is light; in him there is no darkness at all" (1 John 1:5, NIV).

"For God, who said, "Let light shine out of darkness," made his light shine in our hearts to give us the light of the knowledge of God's glory displayed in the face of Christ" (2 Corinthians 4:6, NIV).

"There will be no more night. They will not need the light of a lamp or the light of the sun, for the Lord God will give them light. And they will reign forever and ever" (Revelation 22:5, NIV).

"But you are a chosen people, a royal priesthood, a holy nation, God's special possession, that you may declare the praises of him who called you out of darkness into his wonderful light" (1 Peter 2:9, NIV).

The story of Saul is the story of a man who moved the way he was taught—what he thought was the right way. Then, we learn from Saul's story how he found his true self, his calling, after meeting God. This meeting was so dazzling that he wasn't able to see for three whole days, and that he gained his sight only through the prayer of one of Jesus' followers.

Bible Scripture:

"Meanwhile, Saul was still breathing out murderous threats against the Lord's disciples. He went to the high priest and asked him for letters to the synagogues in Damascus, so that if he found any there who belonged to the Way, whether men or women, he might take them as prisoners to Jerusalem. As he neared Damascus on his journey, suddenly a light from heaven flashed around him. He fell to the ground and heard a voice say to him, 'Saul, Saul, why do you persecute me?' 'Who are you, Lord?' Saul asked. 'I am Jesus, whom you are persecuting,' he replied. 'Now get up and go into the city, and you will be told what you must do.' The men traveling with Saul stood there speechless; they heard the sound but did not see anyone. Saul got up from the ground, but when he opened his eyes he could see nothing. So they led him by the hand into

Damascus. For three days he was blind, and did not eat or drink anything. In Damascus there was a disciple named Ananias. The Lord called to him in a vision, 'Ananias!' 'Yes, Lord,' he answered. The Lord told him, 'Go to the house of Judas on Straight Street and ask for a man from Tarsus named Saul, for he is praying. In a vision he has seen a man named Ananias come and place his hands on him **to restore his sight'"** (Acts 9:1-12, NIV).

Take a moment and offer your insights on these questions:

QUESTIONS

01

02

03

04

05

06

Where are you in life right now, at this moment in time?

_____

_____

_____

_____

What changes have you experienced in your life?

_____

_____

_____

_____

How have you responded to change?

_____

_____

_____

_____

How have you responded in fear of the unknown?

_____

_____

_____

_____

Do you believe that change does not always mean danger?

_____

_____

_____

_____

How can change bring about good in a person's life?

_____

_____

_____

_____

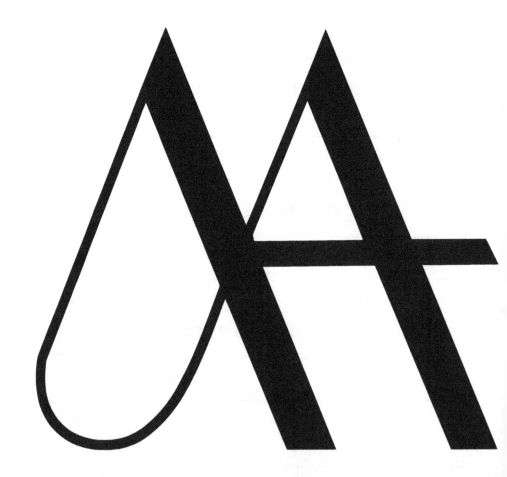

This whole house with many rooms and floors is within us. The unique rooms help us interpret our states and seasons, and they help us interpret where we are in our relationship with God—where He is and where we are.

We take ourselves wherever we go—regardless of the country, or the presence of physical things like houses, apartments, clothes, cars, food, etc. Regardless of whether there are people around us or not, whether we have relatives or not, our inner world is each of us. This is heaven on earth. And for the most part, what heaven on earth will be like for us depends on us. Of course, there are things that we cannot influence, like circumstances, illnesses, and much more; however, we can change our feelings, the ability to believe, hope, move on, and live. We can choose to trust God or not. To grow in faith or not.

We are not strangers to God; we are members of His family, and He can turn any evil into good! There is a lot of evil; no one promised us that on earth we would not meet evil, poverty, disease, and injustice. But we are promised the kingdom of heaven, and life with God on earth, as in heaven. The victory of Christ on the cross gave us this opportunity—on earth as it is in heaven.

This is personal. All people stay in their respective rooms, and no one can see anyone's room but his or her own. Vika could not see mine—what I described in this book. She saw that Jesus was leading me, but He did not show her my rooms.

I invite each of us to enter the house of God, into the rooms prepared for us, to come to ourselves, to the knowledge of ourselves in God—because He is within us.

Bible Scriptures:

"What agreement is there between the temple of God and idols? For we are the temple of the living God. As God has said: 'I will live with them and walk among them, and I will be their God, and they will be my people.'" (2 Corinthians 6:16, NIV)

"Once, on being asked by the Pharisees when the kingdom of God would come, Jesus replied, **'The coming of the kingdom of God is not something that can be observed, nor will people say, 'Here it is,' or 'There it is,' because the kingdom of God is in your midst'"** (Luke 17:20-21, NIV).

"For we know that if the earthly tent we live in is destroyed, we have a building from God, an eternal house in heaven, not built by human hands" (2 Corinthians 5:1, NIV).

This eternal house, your **HOME**, is already inside you.

I invite you to enter it.

ALEKSA AISHPUR'S BIOGRAPHY

Aleksa Aishpur, hails from the vibrant city of Kyiv, Ukraine. With a profound journey spanning two decades, she has seamlessly woven these elements into the fabric of her life, leaving an indelible mark on those she encounters. Aleksa's educational foundation is as diverse as her endeavors. Armed with a Bachelor's degree from the prestigious National University of Kyiv-Mohyla Academy, she is also a graduate of the five teleological christian programs. This comprehensive education forms the foundation of her expertise. In the world of entrepreneurship, her competence is undeniable. She was a co-founder of Ukraine's Crowdfunding platform leveraging her innovative spirit to empower countless initiatives. Her creative spirit also shines through as she masterminded festivals and curated Fashion Shows, breathing life into artistic expressions. As a co-founder of God's Tabernacle with People Church, she weaves spirituality into her dynamic portfolio, fostering a holistic approach to life. Over the past decade, she has been a guiding light, helping individuals navigate the complex terrain of starting businesses, spearheading charity initiatives and realization in life.

During her teenage years, she was involved in ministries with incarcerated youth, children with cancer, people with disabilities and helping people in difficult life circumstances. In 2022, she was involved in communication and teams for humanitarian endeavors across the USA, Ukraine, and Romania, helping widows and rebuilding houses in Ukraine. This diverse skill set encompasses her role as a dedicated jumpstart coach in personal development, business, and career. Her life's mission is to empower others to find their unique path, combining faith, resilience, and purpose to create a brighter future. She is willing to help people find joy in their work and their life. To know more and if you are interested in helpful materials, you can visit her website: http://aishpur.com.

MORE FROM
ALEKSA AISHPUR

What if 'HOME' is not just a physical space where we reside? What if 'HOME' is our entire being?

I'm your Jump-start Coach.

Creator of a method,
I'm here to help you find joy
in your work and life.

WORK WITH ME
A ONE-ON-ONE COACHING SESSION

STEP 1 — Self-Inventory through HOME Framework

STEP 2 — 1-on-1 Coaching Sessions

STEP 3 — Follow-up and Transition Support

Visit my site to explore my unique HOME framework for **FREE** and schedule a coaching session

Made in United States
Orlando, FL
07 January 2024

42185164R00063